Christmas Solos for Students

11 Graded Selections for Intermediate Pianists Arranged by Tom Gerou

This collection contains 11 classic melodies that are frequently requested by students of all ages. *Christmas Solos for Students,* Book 3, is arranged at the intermediate level. Key signatures are limited to two sharps or flats. A maximum of three notes is used for chords played by either hand. Meters of $\frac{4}{4}$, $\frac{3}{4}$, and $\frac{6}{8}$ allow for greater accessibility.

Alfred Music Publishing Co., Inc.
P.O. Box 10003
Van Nuys, CA 91410-0003
alfred.com

ISBN-10: 0-7390-9164-6

ISBN-13: 978-0-7390-9164-7

Cover Art
Christmas background: © istockphoto / Moncherie • Bow: © istockphoto / egal

Away in a Manger

Music by William J. Kirkpatrick
Arr. by Tom Gerou

Bring a Torch, Jeannette, Isabella

Traditional
Arr. by Tom Gerou

Bring a torch Jean - nette, Is - a -

bel - la: Bring a torch, come swift - ly and

run. Christ is born, tell the folk of the

vil - lage: Je - sus is sleep - ing in His

cra - dle. Ah, ah, beau - ti - ful

is the Moth - er. Ah, ah,

beau - ti - ful is her Son.

The Holly and the Ivy

Traditional

Arr. by Tom Gerou

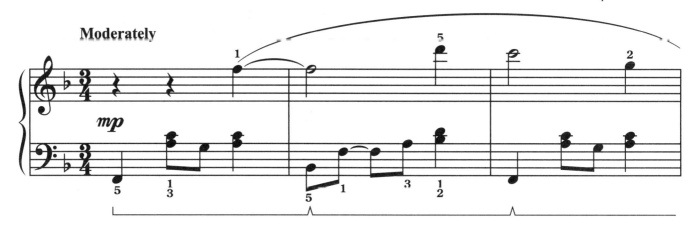

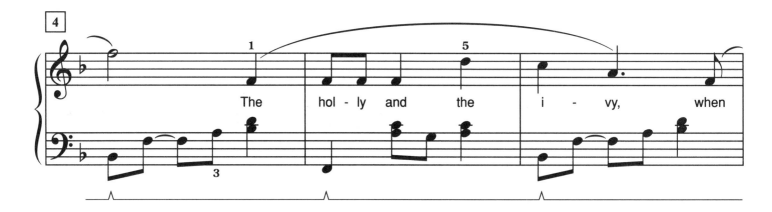

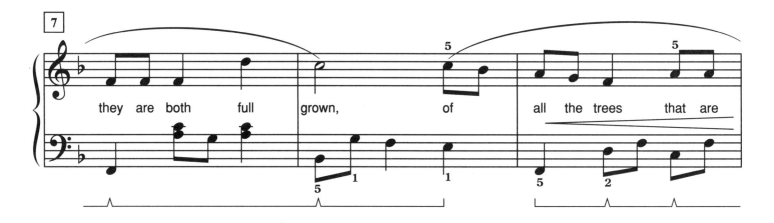

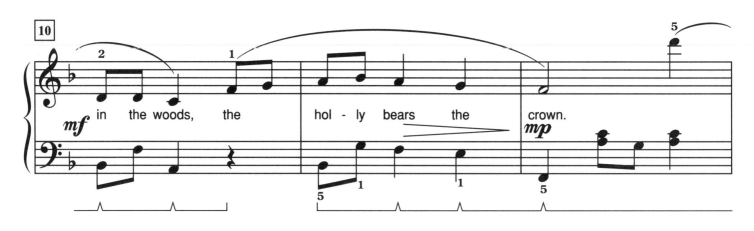

27 hol - ly bears a blos - som as

29 white as li - ly flow'r, and

31 Ma - ry bore sweet Je - sus Christ to *mf* be our Sa - vi -

34 or. *mp*

37 *f* *mf* *p*

The Nutcracker March

Peter Illych Tchaikovsky
Arr. by Tom Gerou

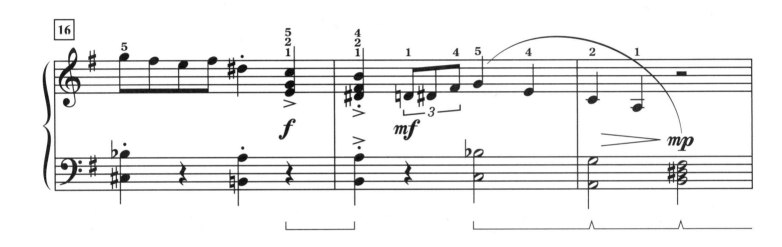

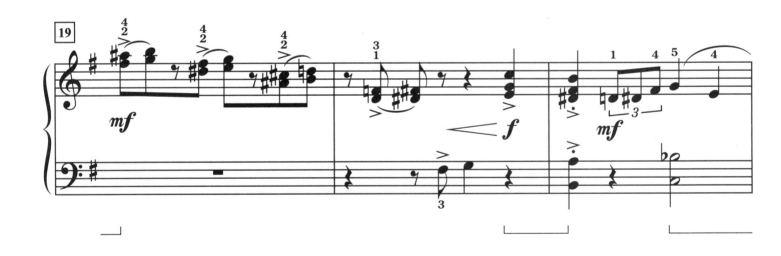

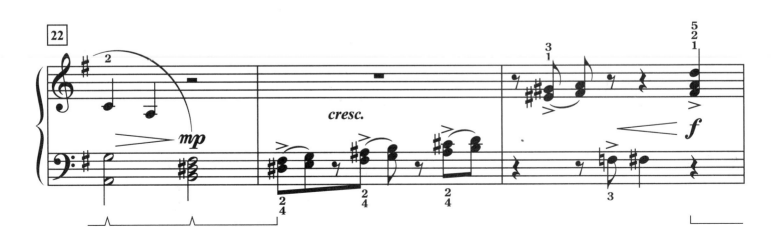

Joy to the World

Words by Isaac Watts
Music by Lowell Mason
Arr. by Tom Gerou

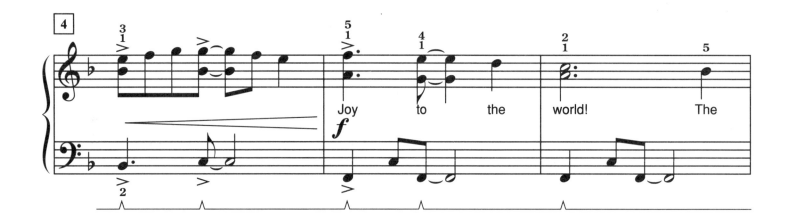

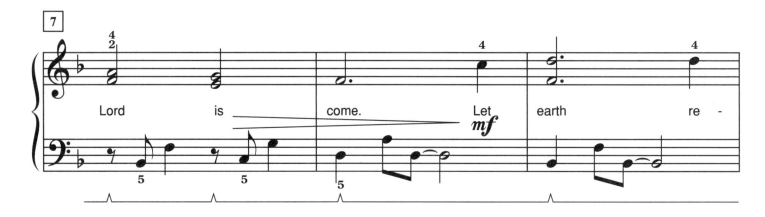

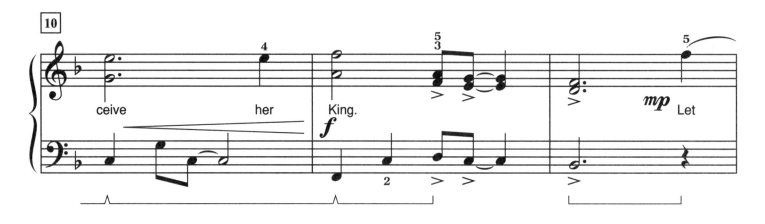

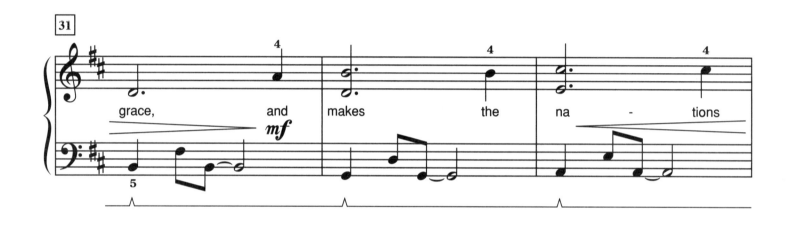

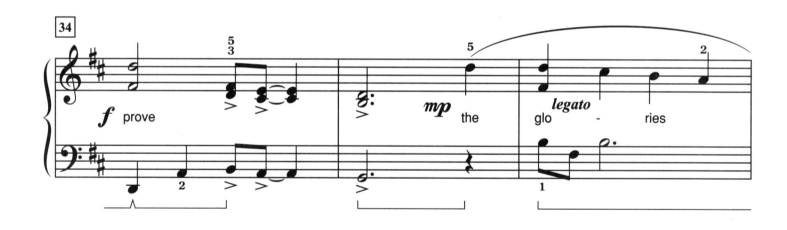

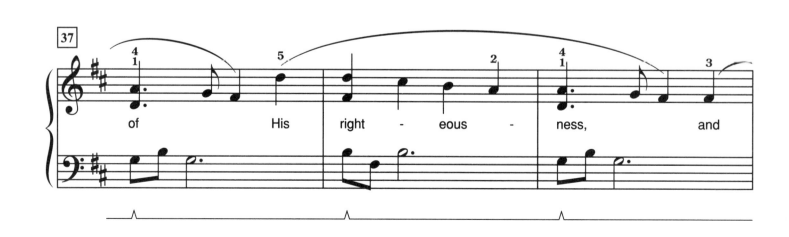

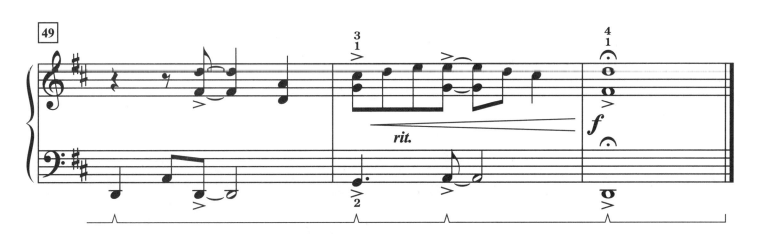

O Christmas Tree

Traditional
Arr. by Tom Gerou

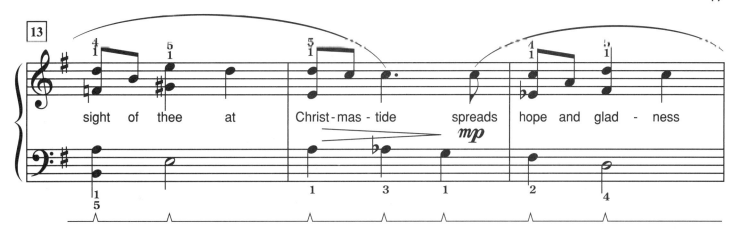

sight of thee at Christ - mas - tide spreads hope and glad - ness

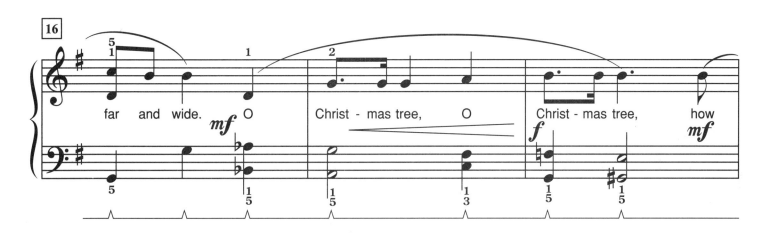

far and wide. O Christ - mas tree, O Christ - mas tree, how

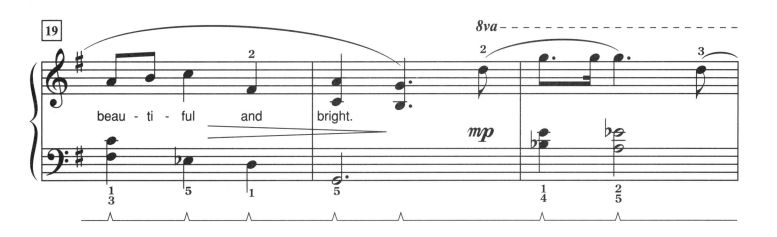

beau - ti - ful and bright.

O Holy Night

Adolph Adam
Arr. by Tom Gerou

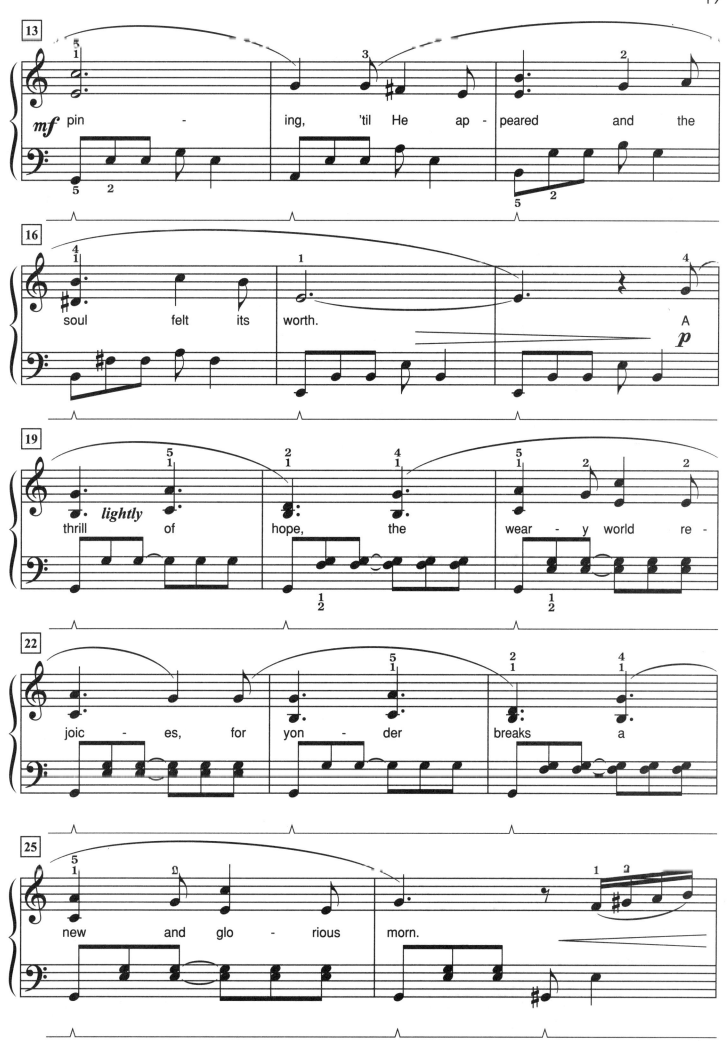

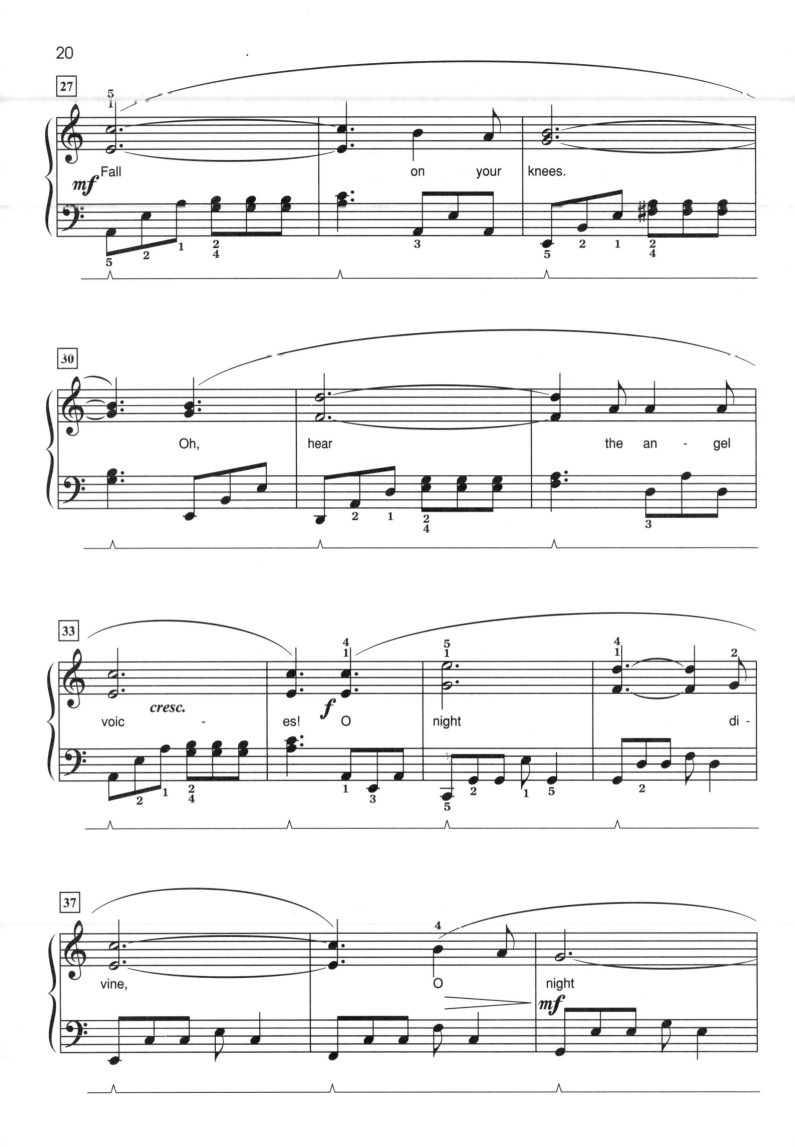

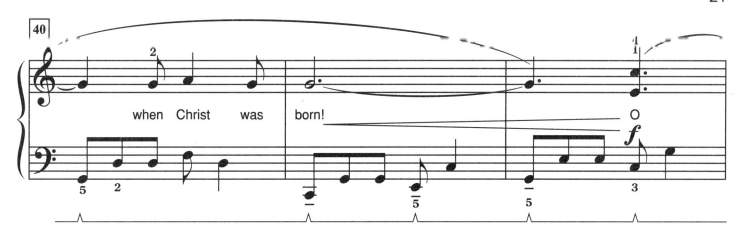

when Christ was born! O

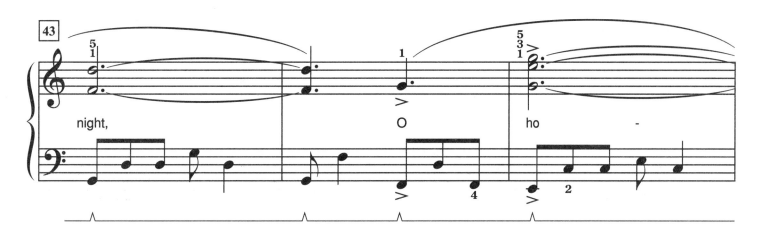

night, O ho -

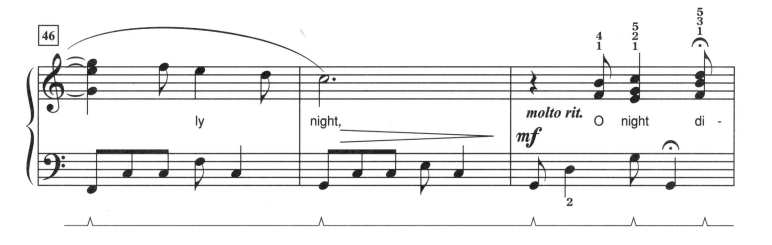

ly night, *molto rit.* O night di -

A little slower

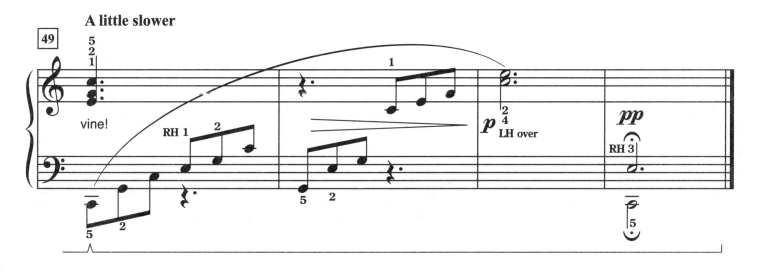

vine!

O Little Town of Bethlehem

Words by Phillips Brooks
Music by Lewis H. Redner
Arr. by Tom Gerou

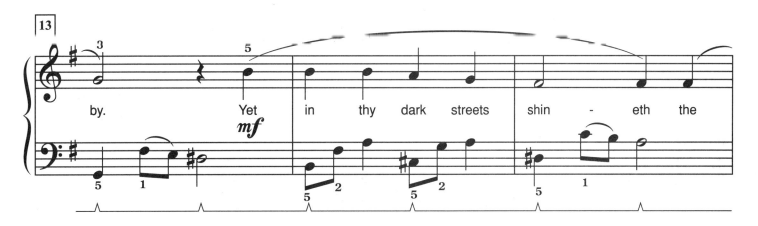

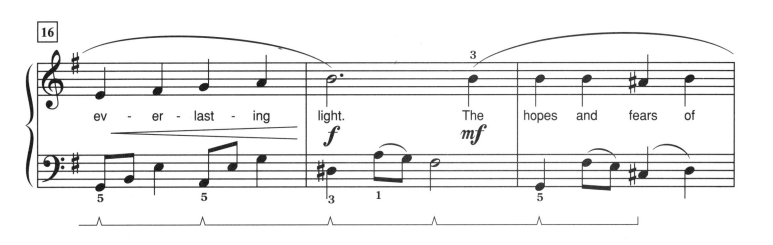

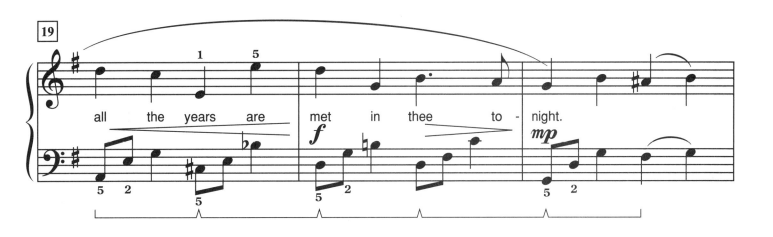

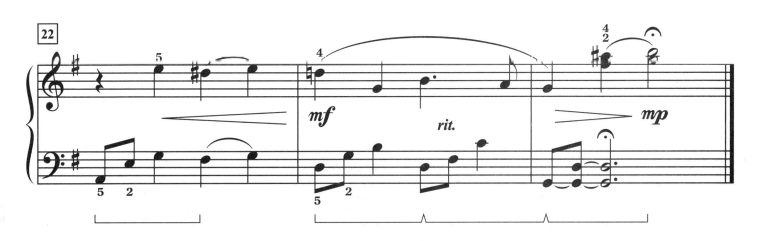

Silent Night

Words by Joseph Mohr
Music by Franz Grüber
Arr. by Tom Gerou

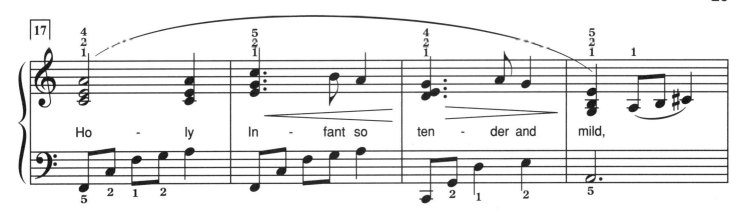

Ho - ly   In - fant so   ten - der and   mild,

sleep   in   heav - en - ly   peace;   *rit.*

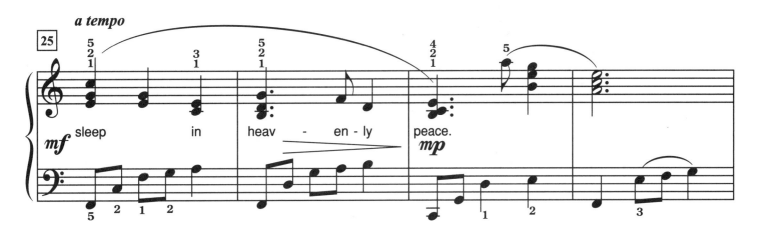

a tempo

sleep   in   heav - en - ly   peace.

rit.

O Come, O Come, Emmanuel

Traditional
Arr. by Tom Gerou

Ukrainian Bell Carol

Mykola Leontovych
Arr. by Tom Gerou

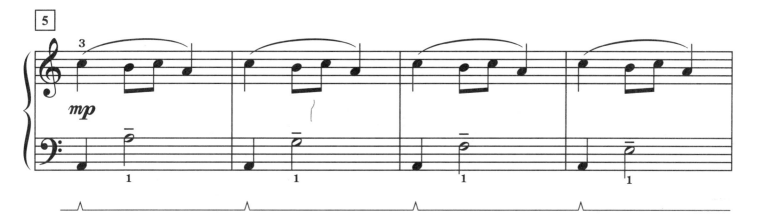

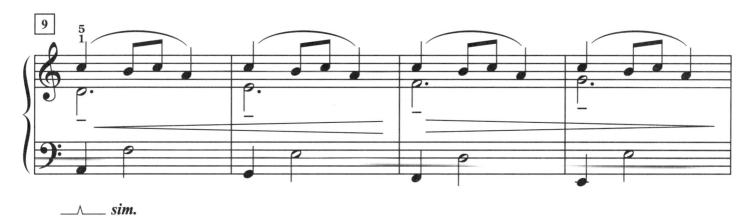

Alfred